Simon,

with love

from all or Tudor.

THE
COMPLETE CLERIHEWS
OF
E. CLERIHEW BENTLEY

The COMPLETE

CLERIHEWS

of

E. CLERIHEW BENTLEY

Illustrated by

NICOLAS BENTLEY
G. K. CHESTERTON
VICTOR REINGANUM

and the Author

With an Introduction by

GAVIN EWART

Oxford New York Toronto Melbourne

OXFORD UNIVERSITY PRESS

1981

Oxford University Press, Walton Street, Oxford OX2 6DP

London Glasgow New York Toronto
Delhi Bombay Calcutta Madras Karachi
Kuala Lumpur Singapore Hong Kong Tokyo
Nairobi Dar es Salaam Cape Town
Melbourne Auckland

and associate companies in
Beirut Berlin Ibadan Mexico City

First published in Great Britain as
Biography for Beginners (1905), More Biography (1929),
and Baseless Biography (1939)

British Library Cataloguing in Publication Data

Bentley, E. Clerihew
The complete clerihews of E. Clerihew Bentley.
1. English wit and humour
I. Title   II. Bentley, Nicolas
III. Chesterton, G. K.   IV. Reinganum, Victor
828'.91209   PN6175
ISBN 0-19-212978-3

Printed in Great Britain by
The Thetford Press Ltd,
Thetford, Norfolk

Contents

Introduction

GAVIN EWART

EDMUND CLERIHEW BENTLEY, famous as the inventor of the clerihew and (to a lesser extent) as the author of the detective story *Trent's Last Case*, was born in London in 1875 and died there in 1956. He was for more than twenty years chief leader-writer on the *Daily Telegraph*. There is quite a long entry concerning him in the *Dictionary of National Biography 1951–1960* and a shorter one, enjoyable for those who appreciate telegraphese, in *Who Was Who 1951–1960*:

BENTLEY, EDMUND CLERIHEW; Writer; *b.* 10 July 1875; *e.s.* of late J. E. Bentley and M. R. Clerihew; *m.* 1902, Violet (*d.* 1949), *d.* of Gen. N. E. Boileau, Bengal Staff Corps; two *s. Educ.:* St. Paul's School; Merton College, Oxford (scholar, B.A.). President Oxford Union Society, 1898; called to Bar, Inner Temple, 1901; joined staff of Daily News in 1902; leader-writer on Daily Telegraph, 1912–34; rejoined staff 1940; writer of detective novels and short stories since 1912; contributor of prose and verse to many periodicals since 1896. *Publications:* Biography For Beginners, 1905; Trent's Last Case, 1912; More Biography, 1929; Trent's Own Case (with H. Warner Allen), 1936; Trent Intervenes, 1938; Baseless Biography, 1939; Those Days, 1940; Elephant's Work, 1950; Clerihews Complete, 1951.

This has the main facts of his life (though he had one daughter who died as a child). His own autobiography *Those Days* and his son Nicolas Bentley's *A Version Of The Truth* (1960) are the two important source books. In fact, the latter tells us a good deal about him, giving life to the bare bones in *Who Was Who*. The son's-eye view is often a clear one.

His father, according to Nicolas, 'was extraordinarily reserved'. 'He was cultivated and widely read, but in most matters of taste he was a Philistine', 'always a stickler for physical fitness', but 'gradually he degenerated into a hopeless hypochondriac, and later on in life he began to hit the bottle'. The cause of this, Nicolas thought, was his failure to get the First in Greats that he expected and to make his mark in the world as his Oxford contemporaries did (Lord Birkenhead, John Buchan).

Nicolas writes: 'I don't remember his ever listening to the radio of his own accord.' Even when bedridden he 'could not be persuaded to look at television'; 'his interest in contemporary literature, particularly fiction, was extraordinarily meagre'. In the latter part of his life he never went to theatres, cinemas or concerts. Nicolas concludes: 'I think it gave him more pleasure than anything else he achieved in life that he lived to see the word "clerihew" . . . enshrined in the Oxford Dictionary as part of our language.'

Bentley's wife, according to Nicolas, suffered from too great a sense of 'family' and was ridiculously proud of being descended from the great French poet Boileau. She called H. G. Wells 'a common little man'. On the other hand, her father, though a General, was charming, intelligent, a radical, a crank and a free thinker; very much in the mould of Anthony Powell's General Conyers, one might think. Thus are the expectations aroused by condensed biography defeated.

Bentley was an intelligent gent – and by this I mean a well-educated member of the English upper classes – liberal and uncensorious in his instincts, a member of the Fabian Society at Oxford (but also an enthusiastic rowing man), born when income tax stood at 2d. in the pound and the British Empire looked as though it would last for ever. But Bentley was very far from being a reactionary jingoist. In his autobiography he wrote, of the Nazis in the 1930s, that they 'pretended, for fear of violence, to believe in a body of pseudo-scientific racial rubbish that is beneath the contempt of every disciplined mind'. At this time there were many Conservatives who regarded the Hitler regime with favour.

In *Trent's Last Case*, published in 1912, the most unpleasant character by a very long way is the murderee Sigsbee Manderson, financier and millionaire capitalist. Julian Symons has pointed out that the detective story writers in the so-called 'Golden Age' of the twenties (Dorothy Sayers, Agatha Christie and Anthony Berkeley in Britain) 'would not have held it against Manderson that he had become rich by speculation'. This social radicalism was inspired by Bentley's old school friend G. K. Chesterton, to whom the book was dedicated. Chesterton later, in 1928, founded the Detection Club, of which he himself was President.

Chesterton was an almost exact contemporary, born one year earlier. When Bentley was twelve he went to St. Paul's, the famous London boys' school, where he met Chesterton for the first time. It was here in 1890, when he was sixteen years old, that Bentley wrote the first clerihew:

> Sir Humphry Davy
> Abominated gravy.
> He lived in the odium
> Of having discovered Sodium.

This was at once illustrated by Chesterton ('abominated' was later changed to 'detested'). The collaboration produced many more. It is interesting that this very first clerihew was never bettered by Bentley. Like a lot of young people's poetry it seemed to come out of the blue, according to Bentley's account. Chesterton wrote clerihews as well (though not one of them is preserved in his *Collected Poems*), and later pursued his draughtsmanship at the Slade School. They remained close friends for the rest of their lives.

First written for fun, as a relaxation from school work, Bentley's clerihews were not published until fifteen years later, in 1905, under the pseudonym of E. Clerihew (his mother's maiden name and his own second name). Bentley wrote, in *Those Days*, that they 'had never a popular success'; he also wrote: 'I never heard who started the practice of referring to this literary form – if that is the word – as a Clerihew; but it began early, and the name stuck.' Clerihews were written, apparently, by James Elroy Flecker and by Charles Scott-Moncrieff. Like the lost plays of Euripides, these seem to have vanished.

At Oxford in the nineties Bentley was fond of P. G. Wodehouse's novels, critical of the hard-drinking lobster-eating nonreading *jeunesse dorée*, but not an 'aesthete'. He was never, I suppose, an extremist. Although he admired Chesterton and Hilaire Belloc – and the latter's best poetry, the *Cautionary Tales*, is light verse of the highest kind – Bentley was not a Catholic. Nor, like them, a Catholic apologist. One clerihew suggests that Bunyan's *Pilgrim's Progress* might be lent to a wicked ogress, and Chesterton's illustration shows the book being posted into a mouth like an enormous letter box. Another concerns Mr. Alfred Beit, who 'screamed suddenly in the night'; no reason is given. Chesterton's picture, however, where Beit is in bed surrounded by moneybags, makes it fairly clear that he is a German–Jewish financier (meerschaum pipe, china tankard, German arms on the wall). The inference is that it was consciousness of the sin of usury that caused him to scream. Bernard Shaw is depicted as a coward, perhaps for his pro-Boer pronouncements:

> Mr. Bernard Shaw
> Was just setting out for the war,
> When he heard it was a dangerous trade
> And demonstrably underpaid.

but this is surprising in a way, since Bentley and his friends regarded the Boer War as a capitalist adventure, with the South

African diamond mines as the prize. In the clerihews Karl Marx is treated with humour, not disapproval. The Primrose League is referred to, obliquely, as an 'unburied ichthyosaurus'. Henry Ford (another millionaire) is satirised for meanness. Political figures such as Snowden, Ramsay MacDonald and Maxton, and American Presidents like Coolidge and Hoover, are not directly criticised for their activities or beliefs. It is all very mild. Even Hitler (*Baseless Biography* was published in 1939) is treated facetiously in the clerihew devoted to Goering:

> 'The moustache of Adolf Hitler
> Could hardly be littler,'
> Was the thought that kept recurring
> To Field-Marshal Goering.

This is mild indeed, considering what Bentley thought of the Nazis. He considered them crude, cruel and bad-mannered compared to the imperialistic militarists of the Kaiser's time, who at least were gentlemen, though of an arrogant and unpleasant sort. Bentley spent a lot of time, as a young man, walking through Europe. He saw the admired German Army at close quarters on manoeuvres and witnessed the worship accorded to it by the civilian population in the years immediately before 1914.

The classical clerihew, then, is free from malice. Bentley probably thought that Beit was a villain, but he doesn't say so. The illustration is far more outspoken; Chesterton was a great arguer and far more of a polemicist. The clerihew could easily be used for satire, and even satire of great bitterness, but as far as I know it never has been. The element of absurdity was there from the first (Sir Humphry Davy), along with the challenge of names that were hard to rhyme, and it belongs to the clerihew – just as jollity, scurrility and sexiness belong to the classical limerick. It's mainly a question of tone, and the tone of the clerihew is both civilised and dotty.

On page 79 of Frances Stillman's extremely comprehensive and useful transatlantic work of reference, *The Poet's Manual and Rhyming Dictionary* (1966), there is the following definition of the clerihew:

The clerihew is named in honor of its inventor, Edmund Clerihew Bentley. It is a humorous pseudo-biographical quatrain, rhymed as two couplets, with lines of uneven length more or less in the rhythm of prose. It is short and pithy, and often contains or implies a moral reflection of some kind. The name of the individual who is the subject of the quatrain usually supplies the first line.

> LOUIS XVI
>
> The Sixteenth Louis
> Exclaimed, 'Phooey!'
> Then, 'Heavens! What was that I said?
> I must have lost my head.'
>
> F.S.

This is a sound definition, except that the 'moral reflection' is often entirely absent in Bentley's pieces. Ms. Stillman's own example makes clear another interesting fact about the form. Nobody much except Bentley has ever written really good clerihews. Even W. H. Auden's *Academic Graffiti* are not satisfactory; in fact they are the least effective poems he wrote.

> My First Name, *Wystan*,
> Rhymes with *Tristan*,
> But – O dear! – I do hope
> I'm not quite such a dope.

This is sad stuff for a major poet. A few are up to the highest Bentley standards, but not many. Two of the best are on Blake and Clough:

> William Blake
> Found Newton hard to take,
> And was not enormously taken
> With Francis Bacon.

When Arthur Hugh Clough
Was jilted by a piece of fluff,
He sighed 'Quel dommage!',
And wrote *Amours de Voyage*.

Anachronism is at the heart of a good many of Bentley's, and Auden has this too; Thackeray is rhymed with daiquiri, for example.

Although the word 'clerihew' has passed into the language, it would still be only a fairly literary kind of person who would know what the word meant. Until quite recently, even in the best dictionaries, there was no entry between 'clerify' and 'clerisy'. Definitions of the word 'limerick', on the other hand and naturally enough, have been offered for a long time.

From the very beginning, even in their early days, clerihews were known to the literate; and now, particularly to the editors of anthologies of light verse, the form is a well-known one. In the American William Cole's *The Fireside Book of Humorous Poetry* (1959) – to give only one example – there is a section entitled 'The Soul of Wit', described as 'an omnium-gatherum of clerihews, epigrams and other pithy pieces'. One can see at once (as the mammoth is the ancestor of the modern elephant) how Blake's epigram on Sir Joshua Reynolds is the true ancestor of the clerihew:

When Sir Joshua Reynolds died
All Nature was degraded;
The King dropped a tear into the Queen's ear,
And all his pictures faded.

This has the right element of fantasy, though it is not mild. Blake means what he says – or implies – that Reynolds was a successful fraud. The metre, though, has something in common with that of the limerick. It is still a rhyming epigram and not a clerihew.

Among the true clerihews that Cole includes (and the majority are the famous ones by Bentley) there are some that reach the required standard:

JACOBEAN

Henry James
(Whatever his other claims)
Is not always too deuced
Lucid.

This is Clifton Fadiman (American).

Massenet
Never wrote a Mass in A.
It'd have been just too bad,
If he had.

This is by Antony Butts (British). Allan M. Laing has a very Bentleian touch:

Samuel Pepys
said it gave him the creeps
to see Nell Gwynn beckoned
by Charles the Second.

and there is a good one by an anonymous writer ('Lakon'):

William the Bastard
Frequently got plastered
In a manner unbecoming to the successor
Of Edward the Confessor.

Ogden Nash, the best modern writer of trivia, never wrote an actual clerihew, though at least one of his epigrammatic comments is very near to one:

THE CANARY

The song of canaries
Never varies
And when they're moulting
They're pretty revolting.

The best non-Bentley work in the genre is by Maurice Hare:

BYWAYS IN BIOGRAPHY

Alfred de Musset
Used to call his cat Pusset.
His accent was affected.
That was to be expected.

Another book that contains very good examples is a rare publication of 1938, *Clerihews*, edited by John Waynflete Carter, printed at the Rampant Lion Press in Cambridge. This describes itself as 'An unofficial supplement to "Biography For Beginners"' and the dedication reads:

In the belief that imitation is still the sincerest
form of flattery, this little anthology is dedicated,
with the diffidence born of admiration,
TO THE MASTER

There is a fine one by Bentley's son Nicolas (his last illustrator):

Cecil B. de Mille,
Rather against his will,
Was persuaded to leave Moses
Out of 'The Wars of the Roses'.

Other good ones are by E. W. Fordham:

Miss Mae West
Is one of the best:
I would rather not
Say the best what.

by John Sparrow:

Sir Lancelot
Used to dance a lot.
None of the dancers
Could beat him at The Lancers.

and by Constant Lambert:

> 'Anthony Adverse'
> May not be bad verse.
> But God knows
> It's bad prose.

There is even what Carter calls 'a discarded child of Mr. E. C. Bentley himself':

> Louis Quatorze
> Had a penchant for wars.
> He sent Turenne to the Palatinate
> With instructions to flatten it.

I was surprised that this modest and beautifully printed little book has a 'cupboard' number in the British Library Catalogue – in other words, it's in with the obscene books. Was Mae West's reputation thought to be in danger in 1938? Italians are referred to in one clerihew as 'wops', there is an uncomplimentary piece about Goering, while another reads:

> The Mikado of Japan
> Is a most extraordinary man.
> He lives in the tops of trees
> Surrounded by Japanese.

It appears, however, that modesty, libel and political expediency were not at stake. Private press books have 'cupboard' numbers too.

Clerihews go on being written. A recent Oxonian anonymity, printed in *The Pelican 1978–79*, has the true Bentley touch:

> Q. Horatius Flaccus
> Wrote an Ode about Bacchus,
> But Bacchus was far too shy
> To write a reply.

I have myself written clerihews, none of which has made me feel particularly proud; this is a recent one:

> Clio
> wasn't happy in Ohio
> and V. Sackville-West and Violet Trefusis
> were more congenial to her than the other eight Muses.

At the moment of writing (December 1980) the current Weekend Competition in the *New Statesman* invites entrants to submit clerihews on existing newspapers and magazines. Bentley's work is a perpetual challenge. Good clerihews have been written since his day; but the inspired lighthearted silliness and unlikeliness of the originals are not easily come by.

GAVIN EWART

Author's Preface

When first it dawned on mankind
Biography for Beginners was signed
(For reasons with which I will not weary you)
With the name of E. Clerihew.

I am not without a claim
To the use of that honourable name,
Which those who happened to be listening
Heard bestowed on me at my christening.

But (for reasons which would only bore you)
The name on the collection* before you
Has been changed—I hope not detrimentally
—To E. Clerihew Bentley.

* These three stanzas began life at the end of
a thirteen-stanza Preface to a new edition of
Biography for Beginners. They appeared in their
present isolation in the so-called *Clerihews
Complete*, which in fact lacked thirty-three of the
previously published specimens (ed.).

Note on the Illustrations

ILLUSTRATIONS which originally appeared in *More Biography* (1929) bear their artists' initials (NB, ECB, GKC, or VR). G. K. Chesterton drew the illustrations to the subjects of *Biography for Beginners* (1905) (Introductory Remarks, Austen, Beit, Belloc, Besant and Rice, Bunyan, Cervantes, Chapman & Hall, Cimabue, Clifford, Clive, Davy, Dewar, Edward the Confessor, Erasmus, Fife, Fuller Acland-Hood, Grieg, Harley, Hirst, Hume, Job, Liszt, Malory, Mahomet, Marconi, Marx, Mill, Odo, Otto, Pizarro, Raleigh, Ricardo, Roosevelt, Shaw, Titian, Van Eyck, Wellington, Werner Laurie, and Wren) and the frontispiece (p. ii), which was originally the front cover of the large-format first edition of that book (in these pictures, when the text refers to the author in the first person, a caricature of Bentley generally appears). All others, originally printed in *Punch* and later collectively published as *Baseless Biography* (1939), are by the author's son, Nicolas Bentley, whose signature in the 'John Knox' illustration—the last of that book —refers to drawings in that whole collection.

Introductory Remarks

The Art of Biography
Is different from Geography.
Geography is about Maps,
But Biography is about Chaps.

'Steady the Greeks!' shouted Aeschylus.
'We won't let such dogs as these kill us!'
Nothing, he thought, could be bizarrer than
The Persians winning at Marathon.

Alexander of Macedon
Became gloomy and taciturn
When they told him at the 'Blue Lion'
That he couldn't have any more Chian.

When a photograph of Attila
Appeared in *The Tatler*
The Huns were all delighted,
And the editor was knighted.

The novels of Jane Austen
Are the ones to get lost in.
I wonder if Labby*
Has read *Northanger Abbey*?

* See Index (ed.).

When their lordships asked Bacon
How many bribes he had taken
He had at least the grace
To get very red in the face.

When the Venerable Bede
Wanted to play Juvenile Lead★
They said they would much rather
He took the Heavy Father.

★ *'Cur non? Quid si prisca redit venus?'*
—*Epistola ad Ecgbertum,* §*127.*

Mr. Alfred Beit
Screamed suddenly in the night.
When they asked him why
He made no reply.

Mr. Hilaire Belloc
Is a case for legislation *ad hoc*.
He seems to think nobody minds
His books being all of different kinds.

Sir (then Mr.) Walter Besant
Would never touch pheasant,
But Mr. James Rice
Thought it *so* nice.

'Corruptio optimi pessima !'
Grinned Sir Henry Bessemer.
'Judicio vulgi demens !'
Snorted Sir William Siemens.

'Sire!' exclaimed Bossuet,
'You are behaving in a gross way.'
'Still, it's rather a lark,'
Replied the Grand Monarque.

Although Don Bradman
Screamed and fought like a madman
And condemned the proceedings *in toto*,
They insisted on taking his photo.

It only irritated Brahms
To tickle him under the arms.
What really helped him to compose
Was to be stroked on the nose.

When Macaulay found Brougham
Sitting on a tomb,
He told his anxious friend
He was meditating on his latter end.

On one occasion when Browning
Saved a débutante from drowning
She inquired faintly what he meant
By that stuff about good news from Ghent.

I do not extenuate Bunyan's
Intemperate use of onions,
But if I knew a wicked ogress
I would lend her *The Pilgrim's Progress*.

Sir Edward Burne-Jones
Was usually Mistah Bones
And imitated a German taking soup
In the Pre-Raphaelite Minstrel Troupe.

'Gentlemen,' said Burns,
'Before the meeting adjourns
I think the least we can do
Is to declare that we are nae fou.'

I fear that King Canute
Was rather a secretive sort of brute.
He would never admit it, but
His name was really Knut.

Thomas Carlyle
Suffered with his bile.
He wrote *Sartor Resartus*;
But that shan't part us.

Lewis Carroll
Bought sumptuous apparel
And built an enormous palace
Out of the profits of *Alice*.

That time when Lord Cecil
Induced Sir Austin to wrestle
Delegates rushed up in a fever
From all over Geneva.

The people of Spain think Cervantes
Equal to half-a-dozen Dantes:
An opinion resented most bitterly
By the people of Italy.

Chapman & Hall
Swore not at all.
Mr. Chapman's yea was yea,
And Mr. Hall's nay was nay.

Geoffrey Chaucer
Took a bath (in a saucer)
In consequence of certain hints
Dropped by the Black Prince.

When they told Cimabue
He didn't know how to cooee,
He replied, 'Perhaps I mayn't,
But I do know how to paint.'

The one thing Cleopatra
Never could abide was a flatterer.
When Antony compared her to Thais
She knocked him right off the dais.

Dr. Clifford
And I have differed.
He disapproves of gin:
I disapprove of sin.

What I like about Clive
Is that he is no longer alive.
There is a great deal to be said
For being dead.

'I quite realized,' said Columbus,
'That the Earth was not a rhombus,
But I *am* a little annoyed
To find it an oblate spheroid.'

The only occasion when Comte
Is known to have romped
Was when the multitude roared, '*Vive
La Philosophie Positive!*'

President Coolidge
Objected to paying muleage
When the people of Nicaragua
Sent him a nice jaguar.

One day the putting of Cotton
Was so indescribably rotten
That H.H. the Sultan of Johore
Beat him by 6 and 4.

Mr. Noel Coward
Was disillusioned and soured
By the lukewarm reception of his comedy
Introducing a real dromedary.*

* Named Ethel.

What if Bishop Creighton
Was descended from a Titan?
A man I know called Binks
Is descended from the Sphinx.

Dante Alighieri
Seldom troubled a dairy.
He wrote the *Inferno*
On a bottle of Pernod.

Sir Humphry Davy
Abominated gravy.
He lived in the odium
Of having discovered Sodium.

Professor Dewar
Is a better man than you are.
None of you asses
Can condense gases.

It was a pity about Dickens'
Insane jealousy of chickens,
And one could really almost weep
At his morbid mistrust of sheep.

A man in the position
Of the Emperor Domitian
Ought to have thought twice
About being a Monster of Vice.

Edward the Confessor
Slept under the dresser.
When that began to pall,
He slept in the hall.

After dinner, Erasmus
Told Colet not to be 'blas'mous'
Which Colet, with some heat,
Requested him to repeat.

It looked bad when the Duke of Fife
Left off using a knife;
But people began to talk
When he left off using a fork.

Mr. Henry Ford
Had a little secret hoard,
To which he would add a dime
From time to time.

'Give me', sang Mr. Fox,
'To wanton with thy locks.'
'That I will never permit!'
Exclaimed Mr. Pitt.

Sir Alexander Acland-Hood
Believed in Free Food:
But he was Eleusinian
About this opinion.

The meaning of the poet Gay
Was always as clear as day,
While that of the poet Blake
Was often practically opaque.

George the Third
Ought never to have occurred.
One can only wonder
At so grotesque a blunder.

'The moustache of Adolf Hitler
Could hardly be littler,'
Was the thought that kept recurring
To Field-Marshal Goering.

Dr. W. G. Grace
Had hair all over his face.
Lord! how the people cheered
When a ball got lost in his beard!

No doubt the poet Gray
Was all very well in his way,
But he couldn't write a song
Like 'Now We Shan't Be Long.'

The musician Grieg
Joined the Primrose League.
It gave him the idea of his chorus,
'The Unburied Ichthyosaurus.'

It is curious that Handel
Should always have used a candle.
Men of his stamp
Generally use a lamp.

It was rather disconcerting for Hannibal
To be introduced to a cannibal
Who expressed the very highest opinion
Of cold pickled Carthaginian.

People wondered why Harley
Sang 'Wae's me for Prince Charlie.'
'It is childish', they said, 'to mourn
For a person not yet born.'

Henry the First
Ate lampreys till he burst.
His unfortunate decease
Simply ruined the Norman peace.

Henry the Eighth
Took a thuctheththion of mateth.
He inthithted that the monkth
Were a lathy lot of thkunkth.

Inspiration visited Herrick
During a mixed foursome at North Berwick.
When his partner had sliced into a drain
He wrote 'To Anthea, Who Gives Him a
Pain.'

When I faced the bowling of Hirst
I ejaculated, 'Do your worst!'
He said, 'Right you are, Sid.'
—And he did.

'Dear me!' exclaimed Homer,
'What a delicious aroma!
It smells as if a town
Was being burnt down.'

President Hoover
Felt in need of a soother
After his little tiff
With Governor Al Smith.

'How many times', mused Hugo,
'Do fours into 372 go?
Come, now; let me see.
I have it—*Ninety-three*!'

That you have all heard of Hume
I tacitly assume;
But you didn't know, perhaps,
That his parents were Lapps.

'Susaddah!' exclaimed Ibsen,
'By dose is turdig cribson!
I'd better dot kiss you.
Atishoo! Atishoo!'

It maddened Dean Inge
To be asked not to sing,*
And there was some savage biting
When they tried to stop him reciting.†

* 'The Gipsy's Warning.'
† 'Zara's Ear-rings.'

Sir James Jeans
Always says what he means;
He is really perfectly serious
About the Universe being Mysterious.

It is understood that Job
Never read *The Globe*;
But nothing could be higher than
His opinion of *Leviathan*.

I doubt if King John
Was a *sine qua non*.
I could rather imagine it
Of any other Plantagenet.

How the Emperor Jovian
Would have revelled in *The Harrovian*!
And can't you see Diocletian
Roaring over *The Fettesian*?

Sir William Joynson-Hicks
Could only count up to six,
Which was rather a wrecker
For his hopes of the Exchequer.*

* Sir William received in 1929 the
consolation of a Peerage of the
United Kingdom under the name,
style, and title of Viscount Brentford,
of Newick in the County of Sussex.

John Keats
Among other notable feats
Drank off a soup-tureen
Full of the true, the blushful Hippocrene.

It was useless to tell a man
So opinionated as Kellerman
That he was absolutely balmy
To think of standing at Valmy.

Dame Laura Knight
Had unusually keen sight.
She could spot a circus clown, they say,
A couple of miles away.

The sermons of John Knox
Teemed with disapproval of frocks.
There was no acquiescence by him in
The Monstrous Regiment of Women.

Archbishop Laud
Saw nothing to admire in *Maud*.
The line he thought most appalling
Was 'Little King Charles is snarling.'

It was a rule of Leonardo da Vinci's
Not to put his trust in princes.
Pleading was of no avail;
They had to pay up on the nail.

The Abbé Liszt
Hit the piano with his fist.
That was the way
He used to play.

Louis the Eleventh
Was contemporary with Henry the Seventh.
I am glad that he
Was not contemporary with me.

Louis Dixhuit
Got decidedly cold feet
When he heard that the Little Man
Had landed at Cannes.

Mr. Ramsay MacDonald
Wished the Channel could be tunnelled.
He said it always got his goat
To be asked if he had lunched on the boat.

Although Machiavelli
Was extremely fond of jelly,
He stuck religiously to mince
While he was writing *The Prince*.

I am not Mahomet.
—Far from it.
That is the mistake
All of you seem to make.

Sir Thomas à Mallory
Always went to the gallery.
He said, not without nous,
That it was the best place in the house.

Guglielmo Marconi
Was brought up on marcaroni,
But when he gets it now
There's no end of a row.

The Empress Maria Theresa
Had a poodle called Sneezer
Which severely bit
A Prussian from Tilsit.

Karl Marx
Was completely wrapped up in his sharks.
The poor creatures seriously missed him
While he was attacking the capitalist system.

As a laddie, Mrr. Maxton
Was apprrenticed tae a saxton.
He thot it wid be prime
To hae Socialism in oor time.

In later life Methuselah
Became a hopeless foozler.
After he was 765
He practically never hit a decent drive.

John Stuart Mill,
By a mighty effort of will,
Overcame his natural bonhomie
And wrote *Principles of Political Economy*.

The digestion of Milton
Was unequal to Stilton.
He was only feeling so-so
When he wrote *Il Penseroso*.

Signor Mussolini
Disliked the name Sweeney.
Anyone bearing it, he said,
Would get a clump on the head.

'Ow!' screamed Beverley Nichols.
'Take it away! It tickles!
You *know* I simply can't bear
An earwig loose in my hair.'

Archbishop Odo
Was just in the middle of 'Dodo',
When he remembered that it was Sunday.
Sic transit gloria mundi.

The great Emperor Otto
Could not decide upon a motto.
His mind wavered between
L'État C'est Moi and *Ich Dien*.

'No,' said Charles Peace,
'I can't 'ardly blame the perlice.
They 'as their faults, it is true,
But I sees their point of view.'

Sir Robert Peel
Said it was not genteel
But, on the contrary, very rude
To tax the people's food.

Peter the Hermit
Neglected to apply for a permit
When raising his mixed brigade
For the First Crusade.

Few Romans were as tony as
The elegant Petronius.
None who dressed snappier
Appeared on the Via Appia.

The views of Pizarro
Were perhaps a little narrow.
He killed the Caciques
Because (he said) they were sneaks.

Although the dialogues of Plato
Do not actually mention the potato,
They inculcate strongly we should
Seek the Absolute Ideal Good.

Edgar Allan Poe
Was passionately fond of roe.
He always liked to chew some
When writing anything gruesome.

'Tiens!' fit M. Poincaré,
'On annonce vingt minutes d'arrêt!
Un coup de vin, qu'il est bon!
Allons! Garçon!'

When Alexander Pope
Accidentally trod on the soap
And came down on the back of his head—
Never mind what he said.

Sir Walter Raleigh
Bickered down the valley.
But he could do better than the rill,
For he could bicker up-hill.

Of course Ranjitsinhji
Was quite right not to be stingy,
But I never could quite see the relevance
Of his keeping nine thousand elephants.

The intrepid Ricardo,
With characteristic bravado,
Alluded openly to Rent
Wherever he went.

If only Mr. Roosevelt
Knew how officers in the Blues felt,
He wouldn't be so rife
With his Strenuous Life.

The poems of Rossetti
Were sweetly pretty,
Especially that one which began,
'Why did you melt your waxen man?'

Rupert of the Rhine
Thought Cromwell was a swine,
And he felt quite sure
After Marston Moor.

Savonarola
Declined to wear a bowler,
Expressing the view that it was gammon
To talk of serving God and Mammon.

Miss Dorothy Sayers
Never cared about the Himalayas.
The height that gave her a thrill
Was Primrose Hill.

I believe it was admitted by Scott
That some of his novels were rot.
How different was he from Lytton,
Who admired everything he had written!

Among the contemporaries of Shakespeare
There were few who regarded him as Drake's peer.
Spoiling paper was so much less strain
Than spoiling the Spanish Main.

Mr. Bernard Shaw
Was just setting out for the war,
When he heard it was a dangerous trade
And demonstrably underpaid.

'No, sir,' said General Sherman,
'I did *not* enjoy the sermon;
Nor I didn't git any
Kick outer the Litany.'

True, Lambert Simnel
Was not an habitual criminal,
But it really was hardly historic
To call himself Earl of Warwick.

Adam Smith
Was disowned by all his kith,
But he was backed through thick and thin
By all his kin.

Mr. Philip Snowden
Was rarely mistaken for Woden.
People as a rule were much more
Apt to mistake him for Thor.

How vigilant was Spenser
As a literary censor!
He pointed out that there were too few *E*s
In Lyly's *Euphues*.

Bishop Stubbs
Was expelled from all his clubs
For disparaging the Oxford crew
In *The Quarterly Review*.

Somebody sent Dean Swift
An ounce of strychnine as a gift.
He took about thirty-five minims
While writing about the Houyhnhms.

As a young man, Tennyson
Wrote a *virelai* about venison,
Which falls into the same group
With his *sirvente* about soup.

When the late Titian
Was in a critical condition,
He was carefully nursed
By Francis the First.

When Torquemada
Found a cat in the larder
He relinquished it without a qualm★
To the Secular Arm.

★ Although its name was Ferdinand.

Sir Herbert Beerbohm Tree
Would never accept any fee
For singing 'The Wearing of the Green',
Accompanying himself on the tambourine.

Martin Tupper
Sang for his supper;
Though the supper wasn't nice,
It was cheap at the price.

That sensitive genius Turner
Simply detested Smyrna.
He said, give him Mozambique
Any day in the week.

The younger Van Eyck
Was christened Jan, and not Mike.
The thought of this curious mistake
Often kept him awake.

It was a weakness of Voltaire's
To forget to say his prayers,
And one which to his shame
He never overcame.

The works of Edgar Wallace,
Were the unfailing solace
Of a recent Prime Minister
When things were looking sinister.

Of all sad words of tongue or pen
The saddest are Captain Wedgwood Benn,
Who, waving aloft his gory sabre,
Placed it at the disposal of Labour.

The great Duke of Wellington
Reduced himself to a skellington.
He reached seven stone two,
And then—Waterloo!

Mr. H. G. Wells
Was composed of cells.
He thought the human race
Was a perfect disgrace.

'Dinner-time?' said Gilbert White,
'Yes, yes—certainly—all right.
Just let me finish this note
About the Lesser White-bellied Stoat.'

hIC : VVILLELM : REX : INTERFEC
TVS·EST

ECB

There exists no proof as
To who shot William Rufus,
But shooting him would seem★
To have been quite a sound scheme.

★ 'Serviit eo hilariter bene recte.'
—Will. Malmesb., *Gesta Regum*, lib. xiv, §329.
'*Porcus lutulentus id certe poposcit.*'
—Eadmer, *Hist. Novorum*, lib. ix, p. 34.

Sir Christopher Wren
Said, 'I am going to dine with some men.
If anybody calls
Say I am designing St. Paul's.'

Brigham Young
Was exceptionally highly strung.
He always used a chopper
When a Mormon said anything improper.

I regard Zinghis Khan
As rather an over-rated man.
What, after all, could be easier
Than conquering from the Pacific to
    Silesia?

Mr. Werner Laurie*
Is not at all sorry
He undertook the publication
Of this instructive compilation.

* Publisher of *Biography
for Beginners* (1905) and
Clerihews Complete (1951) (ed.).

Index of Psychology, Mentality and Other Things

FREQUENTLY NOTED IN CONNECTION
WITH GENIUS

In all work of a biographic character it is important to make copious reference to as many as possible of the generally-recognized virtues, vices, good points, foibles, peculiarities, tricks, characteristics, little weaknesses, traits, imperfections, fads, idiosyncrasies, singularities, morbid symptoms, oddities, faults, and regrettable propensities set forth in the following table. The form of an alphabetic index, with references to the examples given in the preceding pages, has been chosen, so that the beginner who may be desirous, when trying his hand at work of this sort, of seeing how any given one of these subjects may best be treated, is enabled at once to turn to one or more model passages.

Absurdity (GEORGE III)
Allah, Prophet of, refusal to
    admit identity with (MAHOMET)
Amateurishness (ZINGHIS KHAN)
Amnesia (VOLTAIRE, ODO)
Animals, kindness to (MARIA
    THERESA, MARX)
Artistic temperament, the: its
    acute sensitiveness (VAN EYCK);
    love of violent action (LISZT);
    deliberate eccentricity (FIFE);
    naïf self-appreciation
    (CIMABUE); irresistibly attracted
    by the sublime (GRIEG); high
    value set upon it by French-
    men (TITIAN); drunkenness
    (ERASMUS).
Asceticism (MACHIAVELLI,
    SAVONAROLA)
Athenaeum (STUBBS)

Atrocity (WREN)

Backwardness (POPE)
Bankruptcy, moral (WREN)
Bathing, mixed (BROWNING)
Beastliness (RUFUS)
Behaviour, correct (PEEL)
*Beispiel, merkwürdiges, der
    germanischen Individualität*
    (HANDEL)
Bêtise (GEORGE III)
Bodleian, Librarian of the, dis-
    regard for feelings of
    (WALLACE)
Bogey, inferiority to (METHU-
    SELAH)
Bouquet (CHAUCER)
Bullingdon Club (STUBBS)

Catalepsy (TORQUEMADA)

Chagrin (COLUMBUS, COWARD)

Chat, back, propensity for (BESSEMER)

Chelsea Arts Club (STUBBS)

Class (PETRONIUS)

Coevalism (LOUIS XI)

Company, low, penchant for (MALLORY)

Comme il faut, determination to be (PEEL)

Conduct, disingenuous (WREN)

Conviction (JEANS, PEACE, RUPERT)

Coyness (BRADMAN)

Day, rainy, preparedness for (FORD)

Dejection, stanzas written in, nowhere near Naples (MILTON)

Delicacy (BRIGHAM YOUNG)

Diet, indiscretion in (MILTON, HENRY I); morbid delicacy in matter of (DAVY, BESANT, MARCONI, but *cf.* BUNYAN)

Dilettantism (ZINGHIS KHAN)

Domesticity (HENRY VIII, IBSEN)

Domestic servants, dishonesty among, encouragement of (WREN)

Dudgeon (HERRICK)

Eccentric Club (STUBBS)

Efficiency (CIMABUE, DEWAR, HIRST)

Emolument (CARROLL, DA VINCI)

Enjoyment, rational (JOVIAN)

Epilepsy (SPENSER)

Escutcheon, blot on, action involving (WREN)

Excisable commodity, unsympathetic attitude towards (CLIFFORD)

Fact, cynical perversion of (WREN)

Fastidiousness (SHERMAN)

Figure, anxiety about (WELLINGTON)

Flair (KELLERMAN)

Foresight (HARLEY)

Forever young, forever panting and (BEDE)

Frustration (ODO)

Fullness (BURNS, DANTE)

Funereal thoughts, predisposition to (HARLEY)

Gaiters, unfitness for (STUBBS)

Generalisation, sweeping, dangerous fondness for (PIZARRO)

Glamour, negative reaction to (KNOX)

Gourmandise (HANNIBAL, HENRY I, MACHIAVELLI)

Greece, the glory that was, association with (CREIGHTON, HOMER, PLATO); complete indifference to (FORD)

Grundy, Mrs., far-reaching influence of (BRIGHAM YOUNG)

Guile (WREN)

Hair, pigmentation of (RUFUS)

Handicap, length of (METHUSELAH)

Hell-fire Club (STUBBS)

Horrid, dislike of anything (PEEL)

Howler (GEORGE III)

Hypocrisy, calculated (WREN)

Illiberality (COOLIDGE)

Impropriety (PEEL)

Inadequacy (GRAY)

Indirectness (PLATO)

Inexactitude (SIMNEL)

Information, insufficient, proneness to act upon (SHAW, ROOSEVELT)

Insomnia, freedom from (EDWARD THE CONFESSOR); liability to (VAN EYCK)

Integrity, low standard of (WREN)

Ivory, shortage of, immunity from (RANJITSINHJI)

Jehad, interest in, disclaimer of (MAHOMET); involvement in, anxiety to avoid (TURNER)
Jesuitry (WREN)
Jitters (COTTON, LOUIS XVIII); freedom from (AESCHYLUS)
Jockey Club (STUBBS)
Jollity (DANTE)
Jubilee, non-attainment of (HENRY I)
Justification, flimsy, of homicide (PIZARRO)

Klan, Ku Klux, unpopularity among (SHERMAN)
Kleptomania? (PEACE)
Knavery (WREN)

Labouchère, Mr., power to awaken interest in (AUSTEN)
Laicity (HENRY VIII)
Lakhs, separation from (RANJITSINHJI)
Levity, irresponsible, of York-shiremen (HIRST)
Lie, bouncing circulation of (WREN)
Life, high (ATTILA); low (PEACE); wild (WHITE)
Limit, the (STUBBS)
Linen, fine, purple (CARROLL)
Links, frequentation of (COTTON, METHUSELAH, HERRICK)
Love, discouragement of (KNOX)
Loyalty (CHAUCER, ADAM SMITH)

Machiavelli, unholy precepts of, tendency to act upon (WREN)
Manners (PEEL)
Mastication (HENRY I, POE)
M.C.C. (STUBBS)
Mindedness, absent (ODO); broad (PEACE); narrow (KNOX); pure (BRIGHAM YOUNG); strong (CLEOPATRA)
Mirth (JOVIAN)

Nail, tooth and (BRADMAN)
Negligence (PETER THE HERMIT)
Nemesis (TORQUEMADA)
Nests, birds in their little, in-difference to example of (KELLERMAN)
Noblesse Oblige, disregard of apophthegm (WREN)
Norm, departure from the (HANDEL)
Nostrils, reliance upon (HOMER)
Nudism (CHAUCER)
Nuisance (ALEXANDER)
Numbers, Book of, omission from (METHUSELAH); doleful (HER-RICK); inferiority of (AESCHYLUS)

Oeuvre, chef d', objection to (SPENSER); *hors-d'*, love of (POE)
Openness, want of (WREN, CANUTE)
Oriental metaphor, distaste for (CHAPMAN & HALL)
Ostentation (CARROLL, RANJITSINHJI)
Oversight (GEORGE III, PETER THE HERMIT)
Output, literary, miscellaneity of (BELLOC)

Pique (COLUMBUS)
Plantation, de ole, lub ob (BURNE-JONES)
Preoccupation (WHITE)
Principle, lack of (WREN)
Prostration, nervous, freedom from (WERNER LAURIE)
Prudery (BRIGHAM YOUNG)
Psychology, complex and baffling, of contemporary genius (MARCONI)

Publicity (ATTILA)

Quality (ATTILA)
Quandary (GRACE)
Quantity (HENRY I)
Quickening, spiritual, need of
(WREN)
Quietus (RUFUS)
Quotient (HUGO)

Repartee, witty and pungent
(BESSEMER, BOSSUET, CIMABUE)
Resolution (BURNS)
Restoration, lax morality of,
readiness to fall in with (WREN)
Reverie (BROUGHAM, GOERING,
HUGO)
Rome, the grandeur that was,
detraction from (DOMITIAN);
enhancement of (PETRONIUS);
satisfaction with (BELLOC)
Ruin, road to, avoidance of (FORD)

Satanism, revolting display of
(WREN)
Self-effacement, public-spirited
(CLIVE)
Self-respect (PETRONIUS)
Sense of proportion, lack of
(PIZARRO))
Sex-appeal, allergy to (KNOX)
Sheffield Wednesday Football
Club (STUBBS)
Slum clearance, interest in
(HOMER)
Statesmanship, qualities of:
anticipation of coming problems
(HARLEY); readiness to sink own
prejudices in interest of com-
mon weal (ACLAND-HOOD);
freedom from insomnia
(EDWARD THE CONFESSOR)
Superfluity (JOHN)
Surname, non-disclosure of
(PETER THE HERMIT)

Taciturnity (BEIT)
Tactlessness (GEORGE III)
Tailwaggers' Club (STUBBS)
Tat, tit for, aptness in ad-
ministering (BESSEMER)
Tick, refusal of (DA VINCI)
Time, closing, disapproval of
(ALEXANDER); doing, philosophic
approach to (PEACE)
Timing (METHUSELAH)
Tolerance (SWIFT)
Treasury, Parliamentary Secre-
tary to the, anxiety to remain
(ACLAND-HOOD)
Trop, de, openness to suspicion
of being (JOHN)
Turpitude (WREN)

Uffizzi, Palazzo degli, failure to
be persona grata at (DANTE)
Umbrage, quickness to take
(COLUMBUS, ERASMUS)
Unseemliness (GEORGE III)
Unsung, resolve not to be
(KELLERMAN, SHERMAN,
WELLINGTON)
Untruth, plausible, ability to
frame (WREN)

Valhalla, eagerness to qualify for
(SHAW)
Veracity, departure from (WREN)
Victorianism (BRIGHAM YOUNG)
Vitamins, carelessness about
(MACHIAVELLI, TUPPER)
Vivre, savoir (POINCARÉ)

Watchword, ill-chosen, insistence
upon (ROOSEVELT)
Waywardness, discouragement of
(BOSSUET)
Wear, gent's, fastidious taste in
(PETRONIUS, SAVONAROLA)
Whigs, keen party spirit of,
freedom from (FOX)

Width (HENRY VIII)
Wilderness, sojourning in the,
    distaste for (BENN)
Witherin' conventionality, un-
    spiled by (SHERMAN)
Wootton Basset Darts Club
    (STUBBS)
World, the next, neglect of
    prospects in (WREN)

Yahoos, censorious treatment of
    (SWIFT)
Yellowishness (CARLYLE)

Y.M.C.A., unfitness for (WREN)
York, metropolitan see of, dis-
    qualification for (STUBBS)
Youth, mis-spent, evidence of
    (METHUSELAH)

Zealotry (BOSSUET)
Zenith of literary achievement,
    attainment of (AUSTEN)
Zion, outcast from (WREN)
Zulus, table manners of, resort to
    (FIFE)